I Am Who Iamb: An Album of Sonnets

Paul Grossoehme

Presentation by *BookLeaf Publishing*

Web: www.bookleafpub.com

E-mail: info@bookleafpub.com

ISBN: 9789357441544

First edition 2023

ACKNOWLEDGEMENT

It's often said that the act of inclusion necessarily excludes. With that in mind, I hope to give proper due to everyone who influenced me in this project, but I apologize in advance for any omission.

Mrs. Hogan, my high school senior English teacher, started me on this journey. I think it's safe bet that without her this book wouldn't exist.

My fellow tutors in the Learning Assistance Lab in college, especially Laura, Becky, and Naomi, inspired and encouraged my writing during that time.

Ray, my college roommate, was a sounding board on many topics that made their way into sonnet form, and also was the first or one of the first to read many of them.

Jon was another friend from college, a poet in his own right whose prolific output I could never hope to match. He, too, was an encouragement and a spur to me to continue writing.

My wife Christine has been both an inspiration and an encouragement in writing over the years.

Finally in this list but most importantly, God has given me the gift of words. I hope he is pleased with the manner in which I have used it.

PREFACE

I wrote my first sonnet as a senior in high school; it was the last assignment for my English class that year. I found that I was attracted to that specific form and structure and have continued writing sonnets over the years since. The following will provide some background and context to the sonnets found in this book.

"Reflections on a Paper on A Midsummer Night's Dream:" I worked for a semester of my freshman year of college as a peer tutor in the Learning Assistance Lab, where I gained a reputation for being a good proofreader of papers. One of my co-workers asked me to proofread a paper she had written for her Shakespeare class on "A Midsummer Night's Dream" in which one of the sources made the claim that the point of the play was that love was an illusion that one particular woman was different from all the others. That line inspired me to write this sonnet.

"The Lord's Prayer:" I also wrote this as a freshman in college. Unfortunately, the original was lost, but I recalled ten of the fourteen lines and rewrote the ones I couldn't remember.

"Someone Special:" I wrote this for a girl I liked in college. While nothing came of it, I still think it's one of my better works.

"Lonely Lament:" I wrote this as a senior in college to express my frustration with my singleness at the time. When I read it now, it seems just a bit cringeworthy, but no so much that I didn't include it here.

"Magnificat:" This is based on the song of Mary recorded in Luke 1:46-55, commonly called the Magnificat because it is the first word of the song in the Latin Vulgate.

"For Tim on His Wedding Day:" Tim was a friend of mine in high school. We would frequently commiserate as to our lack of success in the romantic arena; in fact, we created a comic strip based on that theme in which we were the main characters. Tim's marriage proved to be a turning point. Tim's Star Trek fandom inspired the last line.

"For Christine . . .:" These three sonnets were written for my wife Christine at various milestones in our relationship.

"Christmas Sonnets:" I wrote these three sonnets as a series one year to put them in the Christmas cards we sent out.

"Last Impression:" This one was born of a somewhat long story from my college years.

During my sophomore year I broke my collarbone playing in a pickup football game. My arm was a in a sling so dressing myself was challenging. In a chapel service shortly after this happened, we were divided into groups to rotate to various stations for prayer. One of these stations was outside, and going out with only a T-shirt on in a Minnesota November was trying. Joanna was one of the others in my group, and when she saw how cold I was, she took her coat off and put it on me. I was not overly surprised as this was the kind of person she was, but it was touching. Little did I know that this was the last interaction I would have with Joanna; she was killed in a car accident that very night.

Those my age or slightly older may remember an old deodorant commercial with the tagline, "You never get a second chance to make a first impression." I thought about that in relation to my experience with Joanna. While it's true enough, first impressions can and frequently are revised with experience with people, but a last impression, like I had with Joanna, can never be changed. What's tricky is that we never know when we're making that last impression.

"Confession:" I wrote this about struggling with sin.

"Immaculate Reception:" I am a lifelong Pittsburgh Steelers fan, and while I was not alive when this play occurred, I am well-versed in its significance in team history. This past winter was the twenty-fifth anniversary of the play in question, and Franco Harris' passing mere days before its commemoration made it that much more poignant.

"Love," "Joy," "Peace," "Patience:" These are the first four virtues listed in the fruit of the Spirit as recorded in Galatians 5:22-23

"Thoughts on Competitiveness:" Throughout my life I've been a competitive person even in the most casual or friendly of games, and I've often been frustrated by other people's reactions to this.

"Reflections of an Introvert:" I have an introverted personality and this sonnet examines themes common to many of us who would describe ourselves in this way.

Reflections on a Paper on A Midsummer Night's Dream

They told me that it was foolish of me
To think that one girl stands above the rest.
They say I am deceived by what I see;
It's only an illusion, they attest.

"There is no difference in womankind;
A man is only by his passions seized."
On hearing them, I took their words to mind
To test them fully with my faculties.

They say my eyes and mind do play a game,
But in my heart I know it isn't true,
For if all women truly were the same,
How could there be one wonderful as you?

So let them taunt and let them criticize.
I see you; I know I can trust my eyes.

The Lord's Prayer

Our God and Father, who in heaven art,
Most high and holy we declare your name.
The One who is the ending and the start,
Immutable -- from age to age the same,

Your kingdom come; your will be done on earth
Just as it is performed in heaven's sphere.
We long to serve you, giver of new birth;
Pour down your Spirit's power on us here.

Provide our daily bread and lift our cares;
Forgive our sins as others we forgive,
And help us guard against the tempter's snares.
Deliver us from evil as we live.

All power, glory, and authority
Be yours forevermore! So let it be.

Someone Special

Here in a space of solitude I find
Some time to contemplate and to reflect,
And in my passing thoughts you come to mind
As one whom I admire and respect.

When gazing on your lovely eyes of blue,
I could at times just sit and stare awhile.
There is a certain radiance in you;
The whole room seems to brighten when you
smile.

That visage that illuminates my day
Reflects, I hope, the joyfulness inside;
And if my face my feelings would betray,
These humble penstrokes couldn't be denied.

So on this day I wish for you to see
I think that you're of special quality.

Lonely Lament

My heart desires another human heart
Its longings and its fears with which to share;
To whom its deepest secrets to impart.
I'm trapped within a life that isn't fair.

For in her eyes the heart is little seen;
My character is given scarce regard.
'Tis toward the external that she leans,
The surface trappings with which some are
starred.

My quandary of being dealt low cards
To quite a few a man has been attached.
A heart of gold won't get him very far
Unless he has a face of gold to match.

I'm thus consigned to anonymity,
To walk this road with none for company.

Magnificat

My soul within me glorifies the Lord;
My spirit in my Savior God takes joy.
My humble state he has not left ignored;
He chose me for his purpose to employ.

The generations all will call me blessed;
The Mighty One has done great things for me.
He makes his tender mercy his bequest
To those who fear him, for eternity.

His mighty arm has brought about great things;
He scatters the conceited and the proud.
He humbles and dethrones the greatest kings,
Remembering the promises he vowed

To Israel, the house of Abraham,
To all who call upon the great I AM.

For Tim on His Wedding Day

It sometimes happens as a chapter ends
I find it difficult to turn the page.
I know that as life's pathway turns and bends,
We come and go, as actors on the stage.

As we've been friends for oh so many years,
Appreciation for that bond has grown;
Our laughter oftentimes brought us to tears,
The craziest that I have ever known.

And yet the magnitude of this great day
Somehow eludes the words that I employ;
Remembering our best of times, I pray
That you would come to find the greatest joy.

May God above keep love forever true;
May you live long, and may he prosper you.

For Christine
Commemorating Six Months Together

The road of life can leave the mind perplexed
When somehow your desires are realized.
Just when you think you know what's coming next,
A twist will leave you pleasantly surprised.

My past affections, pensively recalled,
Were marked with bitter angst, left unfulfilled;
To some degree I find myself appalled
To find these feelings once again instilled,

For all the things you mean to me outweigh
My penchant to express all that is due;
Above all, this is what I want to say:
I hope that I can be the same for you.

So always in my memory I'll store
These cherished days, and hope for many more.

For Christine on Our First Valentine's Day

These days of winter, dark and gray and cold,
Have mirrored all too well my present state.
My patience and endurance have been tolled
Without hiatus or reprieve of late.

Yet still my faith, though wavering, still clings
To hope that God has not forgotten me,
For through the balance of all living brings,
I can't see him, but you, my love, I see.

Aside from all your many pleasing charms
And all the many moments of pure bliss;
Beyond the thrill of you snug in my arms
Or sharing an incredible sweet kiss,

I value you because you are God's face,
Prepared for me for just this time and place.

For Christine on the Anniversary of our Engagement

Considering you, whom I would not trade
For any other, so therefore I wed:
To say to you, "I love you," should be made
A habit, though not out of habit said,

For saying such reflexively would be
To take for granted all you freely give,
And that, because of all you mean to me,
Would be a grievous error down to live.

For I'm convinced within my heart and mind
That 'twas for me that God created you,
So gentle I resolve to be, and kind;
To be compassionate, to love so true.

To this I am obliged, though not to keep
Of obligation, but a love so deep.

Christmas Sonnet #1

Across the landscape's scope, the decked-out
halls
Are covered with a superficial glitz,
And stores of every size and shopping malls
Play host to a most overwhelming blitz.

Short tempers flare; the myriad demands
Leave all the parties in their wake unnerved.
Observing all the mammon changing hands,
I wonder -- just which master's being served?

Unfolding scenes, so many toils and cares --
They make a mockery of "peace on earth;"
They seem so small when only one compares
The wonderment of God's incarnate birth.

Today, and all year long, may we recall
That Jesus is the meaning of it all.

Christmas Sonnet #2

Four centuries of silence, dark and cold
Had passed without prophetic word nor sign.
The desperate, weary world would soon behold
In human face, the countenance divine.

Although he the whole universe sustained,
He came into this world unrecognized.
His rightful adoration not attained;
Instead he was rejected and despised.

He pitched his tent among us, none too late,
To penetrate the darkness with the light;
Mankind to rescue from his fallen state,
So he could be a child of God by right.

The gift belongs to all who will receive,
And in the name of Jesus Christ believe.

Christmas Sonnet #3

Completed with God's very breath inspired,
Mind, spirit, soul, and body all in tune;
The human race God's image so acquired,
With God himself created to commune.

But man's offense communion severed twain,
A toxin that no antidote could quell.
His earthly life left purposeless and vain,
Condemned to an inevitable hell.

His Maker, the embodiment of love
Death's cruel certainty could not abide,
So he forsook the paradise above
And took on flesh, and for the creature died.

The greatest gift is God's own wondrous grace
To take the punishment in mankind's place.

Last Impression: In Memory of Joanna

It's said one never gets a second chance
A first impression on someone to make.
In order a poor picture to enhance,
Excessive labor oftentimes would take.

Although the former adage truly spoke,
Your last impression's one you'll never see,
And it can never truly be revoked;
It leaves its mark throughout eternity.

The choice to be indifferent or be kind
Is written with a lifetime's ink and quill.
A burden great weighs heavy on the mind --
That impact on a life, for good or ill.

Thus 'tis my prayer that others always see
Divine reflections flowing out of me.

Confession

Considering the darkness I've indulged,
My soul is wracked with frightful turbulence.
My guilty secrets ne'er to be divulged
Leave not a minute trace of innocence.

The fleeting pleasure my rebellion brings
Cannot withstand the trauma that ensues.
I see the cold exchange for sinful flings:
For brief delight, there's everything to lose.

But God is just and faithful to erase
All manner of transgressions I confess.
His blood cleans everything I couldn't face;
It works my sore condition to redress.

Amazing grace! It broke the chains that bound;
I once was lost, but now, praise God! I'm found.

Immaculate Reception

The Steelers, in a playoff game so rare,
They bore the weight of twoscore futile years.
The great anticipation in the air
Was intermingled with well-founded fears.

Despite a narrow lead maintained throughout,
So many waited for it to be blown.
The late fourth quarter justified the doubt,
And disappointment would retain its throne.

On fourth and ten from sixty yards away,
A desperate pass defensed, apparently,
But it was rescued on the ricochet,
And carried all the way to victory.

If ever just one play reversed a fate,
'Twas that one which is called immaculate.

Love

The question, "What is love?" persists to show
Though generations take its depths to plumb.
So many hearts and souls purport to know;
We are by our emotions overcome.

The heart pursues, regardless of the pain;
In gaining of control we lack success,
But over time, euphoric feelings wane.
Such love divorced from will is meaningless.

While down infatuation's path we're led,
Our only object just ourselves to please,
The Lord's example turns it on its head;
He died to save his bitter enemies.

So oft we're unprepared to pay the price,
But perfect love equates with sacrifice.

Joy

When I observe the world that is today,
It seems there's little respite from great care.
It's plain to see the rational decay;
The wider road's a highway to despair.

The pseudo-moral bullies of the left
Have overtaken what is just and true;
Besieged, we weary brothers lack the heft
To run our culture backward from this zoo.

The joy of which we speak, where is it found?
How, in the present days, are we to cope?
Though adverse circumstances still abound,
We "set our minds on things above" with hope.

The end's already written, and we know
We have the victory o'er things below.

Peace

Within our lives, and broader out beyond,
The conflicts and the worries never cease;
For efforts at resisting to despond,
We've never needed more the Prince of Peace.

Our leaders promise ending to the strife;
It seems they never cease to disappoint.
The friction is a constant part of life,
No matter who we take up to anoint.

The peace that Jesus promises to give
Outstrips the human mind's capacity.
Through daily tumult we may have to live;
In him we've unsurpassed tranquility.

Though all around the stormy ocean rolls,
The quiet river babbles in our souls.

Patience

Frustration's clutches seldom seize me more
Than facing checkout lines or traffic lights.
The world's inclined completely to ignore
Exaggerated concepts of my rights.

To put minute annoyances aside
Provides sufficient challenge for my flesh,
To mention nothing of respect denied,
And larger, greater injuries afresh.

To wait, perhaps, is e'en more tiresome when
God's plan I deem too slowly has progressed.
The schedule's his; he answers not to men.
I must recall his timing is the best.

As long as I'm encamped in body here,
My way is his and I will persevere.

Thoughts on Competitiveness

I must confess I fail to understand
Prevailing attitudes on sportsmanship,
Dictating that participants withstand
Adversity without emotive flip.

When someone says, "We only play for fun,"
I scarce can undertake to shoulder blame
As sharply does my disagreement run:
As Edwards said, "You play to win the game!"

For those who can take pleasure through a loss
I muster no regard nor sympathy.
I would to rubbish such opinions toss;
The sportsman seen reduced to apathy.

When will my view evolve from being crass?
When porcine aviation comes to pass.

Reflections of an Introvert

Outgoing people seem to have the fun;
Few people would dismiss the party scene,
But still when everything is said and done,
The social crowds will find me less than keen.

Good friendship is a blessing all its own,
But company is not without a catch.
The opportunity to be alone
Provides a solace nothing else can match.

A hermit or a recluse I am not;
All equal, I prefer my inner voice,
To spend an hour or two absorbed in thought
Or quiet entertainment of my choice.

The extrovert may many more friends make,
But depth for numbers is a trade I'll take.